T0193889

AUTHENTIC TESTIMONY

WALKING IN MY SEASON OF AUTHENTICITY

ROYAL CHATMAN

authorHOUSE®

AuthorHouse™
1663 Liberty Drive
Bloomington, IN 47403
www.authorhouse.com
Phone: 1 (800) 839-8640

Published by AuthorHouse 10/18/2019

ISBN: 978-1-7283-3171-3 (sc)
ISBN: 978-1-7283-3170-6 (e)

Library of Congress Control Number: 2019916449

Print information available on the last page.

Any people depicted in stock imagery provided by Getty Images are models, and such images are being used for illustrative purposes only. Certain stock imagery © Getty Images.

This book is printed on acid free paper.

Because of the dynamic nature of the Internet, any web addresses or links contained in this book may have changed since publication and may no longer be valid. The views expressed in this work are solely those of the author and do not necessarily reflect the views of the publisher, and the publisher hereby disclaims any responsibility for them.

CONTENTS

PREFACE

Father, I ask that You bless the reader of this book. I ask that You release the comfort of Your presence and Holy Spirit upon each person so that he or she may experience Your serenity through the humility of Your willing servant.

I want to take this moment to engage you, the reader, the one whose eyes are soon to gaze upon the pages of this book. My hope is that you not only read this book but also allow for the passion of the author to not be mere words, taking it with a grain of salt. I would like to first engage you with a dear and near scripture of mine, Colossians 4:6. "Let your speech at all times be gracious and pleasant, seasoned with salt." For this very reason, I have been blessed with the gracious words that you will find within the pages of this book, and I wish to impart the granted words of wisdom and life to enlighten those who find themselves gazing upon the very pages of this book of authenticity.

Now, Father, I ask that You humbly receive all that I write and impart the triumphs, adversities, and trials of afflictions. Share all the broken pieces that You have taken upon Your love and put them back together. Make a testimony and let it be a reflection unto them so that all brokenness can be put back together if it is returned to the Potter's hand. Make it so that it will be used for Your will and glory. Amen.

ACKNOWLEDGMENT

I truly thank God first. He has allowed me another opportunity to write, share, and express the many encounters I have had in both my life and my life incarcerated. I give all glory to Him because it would not be possible to have lived my life without the tremendous amount of mercy and grace that He has given unto me through the sacrifice and love of His Son, Jesus Christ. Honestly, there is no other way I can or need to put it. There is no other reason that I am breathing today. There is no other reason that I am alive and free today. For that, I choose to give honor to whom it belongs. I will not place anyone or anything else upon this page because it is by Him that I present unto you.

Thank You, Lord Jesus!

CHAPTER 1

A Shift of a Season

I, the author, invite you, the reader, the one whose eyes gaze upon the pages that are within the chapters of this book, to be inspired and to find yourself encouraged. Surely, I hope to motivate so that by the end of this book, readers will find themselves highly charged and in a position to become authenticated.

Let me enlighten you of the shifted season that the Lord presently has in my life. I owe this book dedication to January 15, 2018. I remember so well the day the Lord brought me humbly to my knees. This is dated well beyond January 15, 2018. There is power in testimony—not only in testimony but in the words of your testimony. The problem I find is that there are not too many sharing that God-given power of a testimony. First, I believe it is because many have not become confident in the One who has given them the testimony. Second, I believe many are spending too much time comparing stories instead of identifying a testimony. I mean, how many times have we pushed so many things to the side as if there is no significant value to them? How many times has God showed up and showed out in your life, only to have it pushed to the side? No biggie, Lord. That death that You just spared me from is no biggie. That cure from that deadly sickness or disease? No biggie, God.

Many are going through life with the attitude that they deserve everything that comes their way—good, bad, or indifferent. Well, enough is enough.

Have you found yourself in any of the following categories?

1. "My life has no meaning."
2. "I know that I am meant to be something. I just don't know what that is yet."
3. "If I only had this or that, things would be better."

These are just a few of the excuses that we choose to use or come up with, never wanting to face the truth that change is needed, and that change can be fearful and challenging.

I am reminded of these great words a wise man said to me: "Are you a host to your faith, or a hostage to your fears?" Wow! These divine words of wisdom caused me to pause and meditate. These are the moments in which we need to remind ourselves that God has not given us the spirit of fear but of power and love, as well as a sound mind.

It is my deepest prayer that this book makes you question the authenticity of your own walk of faith, starting with the road that you are presently on. It is written,

> Enter by the narrow Gate; for wide is the Gate and broad is the way that leads to destruction, and there are many who go in by it. Because narrow is the Gate and difficult is the way which leads to Life, and there are few who find it. (Matthew 7:13–14 NKJV)

There is going to come a point in our lives when God is simply going to shift our season. There are times when we may not realize that God has been on the move, preparing a new season for our lives. But at times, we have not shifted with God in this newly prepared season because we have become comfortable with the season that we are presently in.

I have to pause and fill you in as I am writing these words to you. I found myself sometimes lingering around the familiar season of comfort that I was in. I was more relaxed with the way things were going. The people God had allowed to come into my season never wanted to shift out of that comfort zone until God finally came and uttered these soul-touching, heartfelt, "still small voice" words to me: "Royal, where are you?" It was alarming at first because I always felt that I was in the perfect will of the Lord. I was somewhat confused.

At this point, I must be the first to say to you, "Let

us take off our holier-than-thou hat, and let us come to the agreement that we at times could have some stinking thinking going on at times."

"My thoughts are not your thoughts, nor are your ways My ways," says the Lord. "As the heavens are higher than the earth, So are My ways higher than your ways, And My thoughts than your thoughts." (Isaiah 55:8 NKJV)

As I stated, I thought that I was in the perfect center of His will before I heard the Lord utter, "Royal, where are you?" I proceeded to answer with what I thought was feasible, but He replied, "Why are you there?" Now I became more confused, and to be honest, I was slightly angered. I felt I was doing everything right regarding all that He asked of me. I saw somewhat great change and growth in areas. Let's be honest: sometimes we are so convinced that the place we are at is where God wants us to be. Come on! How many times have we said to ourselves and others, "God has got me in a good place of my life," only to have such a statement from a preconceived notion? Well, the point I am trying to reach is this:

> Trust in the Lord with all your heart and lean not on your own understanding In all your ways acknowledge Him In all your Ways And He shall direct your paths. Do not be wise in your own Fear the Lord and depart from evil. (Proverbs 3:5–7 NKJV)

If God is not the director of all your steps, then that one step without Him directing makes all the other steps in vain. God had come to share with me, "Royal, I am no longer in that season of your life. I have shifted your season, and no matter how comfortable that season may have been for you, I need for you to shift into the season of newness. You have no idea that the season that you are comfortable in is on the verge of destroying you. But there are times when God will revisit His son or daughter and ask, 'Where are you?'"

Adam was given the same question right after disobeying God's commandment. Adam's season had shifted. Not once did Adam seek to call out to God and understand what he had just seen regarding the difference of Eve after partaking of the forbidden fruit. Yet he and Eve, his wife, were willing to remain in a state of not only rebelling in that falling state but seeking to make that tainted season comfortable by sewing fig leaves. They never came to the realization that the season that he was seeking comfort in was about to destroy him.

Then we see the beauty of God's display of grace and mercy appear in a small, still voice uttering, "Adam, where are you?" At that moment, we find God seeking His fallen son and daughter and revealing to them that He was preparing for them a shifted season.

Out of all the choices of disobedience and rebellion, where are you, reader? On the opposite side of this page, write your thoughts.

Hebrews 3:15 (NKJV) says, "Today, if you will hear His voice, Do not harden your hearts as in the day of rebellion."

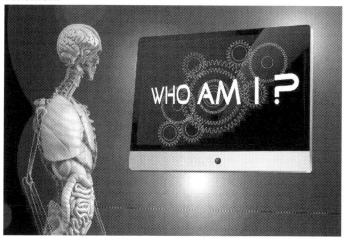

Is God calling you from a season of comfort? Is He calling you from a season of rebellion? He may be calling you from a season of disobedience, which leads to destruction. He is calling you to a season of preparation and purpose. I believe the words within this book will challenge you, motivate you, and inspire you to examine the season that you are presently in and ask yourself this one simple question: "Am I comfortable?" If the answer is yes, then I caution you to call on your loving, heavenly Father and say, "Father, am I pleasing in Your sight? Or has my comfort distracted me and somewhat hindered me from hearing Your call of instruction to shift into a newly prepared season of purpose that You have prepared in Your wisdom?"

We must be careful. Many people may be using their gifts and talents in places of their own choosing and not in the places of the Lord's choosing. Yes, I know it may seem right, and it may also look and feel right. But neither of these descriptions is permitted by God.

> There is a way that seems right to a man, But the end is the way of death. Even in laughter the heart may sorrow, And the end of mirth may be grief. The backslider in his heart will be filled with his own ways," But a good man will be satisfied from above. (Proverbs 14:12–14 NKJV)

Let us not forget 2 Corinthians 5:7, which says, "For we walk by Faith, not by Sight." Most assuredly, we are not to allow our carnal thinking to lead us to carnal living.

CHAPTER 2

WALKING IN MY SEASON OF AUTHENTICITY

Are you walking out of your season of rebellion, or have you found your steps and conversation leading nowhere? God wants to take His words of life within this book and walk you out of any season, whether it's rebellion, unforgiveness, bitterness, pride, haughtiness, unloving, or uncaring. Whatever season it may be, God wants to use this very valley of season and begin to authenticate a testimony within you. Get ready, tears, to say goodbye. Get ready, fears; you are no longer welcome here. Get ready, hopelessness, to hope again. Get ready, insecurities, to say goodbye. But don't you go too far because God is about to use each and every one of my hindrances, trials, and life challenges, and He is about to turn it around for His glory and my good.

> And we know that all things work together
> for the good to those who Love God, to those

who are called according to His purpose. For whom He foreknew, He also predestined to be conformed to the image of His Son, that He might be the first born among many brethren. Moreover whom He predestined, these He also Called; whom He called these He also Justified; and whom He justified these He also glorified. (Romans 8:28–30 NKJV)

Are you at a point in your faith walk that you find it uncomfortable sharing with others what God has brought you through? Well, please don't feel alone. I remember the time when I was trying to make some sense of how the Lord could have chosen me out of all the other grand people. I thought surely He could have found a better candidate. I mean, He chose this former drug dealer who was highly prideful and overconfident. At time arrogance got the best of me, but I truly wrestled with the fact that He'd chosen a wretch like me to share my story, and at first I remember asking the Lord, "How about using someone else?" Have you ever uttered such words only to get a response?

He said to me, "Where you see trash, I see treasure. Where you see hurt, I see a church. Where you see pain, I see gain."

Simply put, our lives have so much meaning and purpose, and no matter how much we don't understand it, God knew why He called you. He also knows everything He called you from, and He is going to use it all for a greater purpose of His glory. He'll use you right where you are. I mean you, the reader. Yes, you! Don't look around—I am talking to you who have just read the last few words upon this page. Right where you are at this moment, I want you to turn around. If you are sitting, stand up! If you are in the line at the department store, I don't care; I want you to turn around. It is a new start in a new direction. It is a fresh turnaround to your circumstances. It is a bold step of getting out of the familiar and being ready to take steps in the newness. I am ready for you to take a step toward not allowing the cares of this world to weigh you down so that you lose your joy. Turn around because in your turning, you show every lying tongue, every weight of the enemy, and every depressing thought from the enemy that God is about to use it for your good. You see, the hidden power is within you. I will say it again: the hidden power is within you

> You are Of God, Little Children and have overcame them because greater is He that is within you than he that is in the world. (1 John 4:4 NKJV)

I know many of us believe that when you start talking about powers within you, some people think about Power Rangers, Superman, the Hulk, or some other hero. But there is a hidden power in so many, and there has been given a power within many of us. The only problem is many of us are not using this given power. Why? Because some have not realized that it exists within them, and others have become distracted and amazed by this power in someone else, not knowing that they also possess the same hidden power.

> Verily, verily, I say unto you, He that believeth on me, the works that I do shall he do also; and greater works than these shall he do; because I go unto my Father. (John 14:12 KJV)

I am about to unlock a door to your season. Notice that I did not say a secret door. God is ready for you to say so!

Let the Redeem of the Lord Say So, Whom He has redeemed from the hand of the enemy. And gathered out of the of the lands from the east and from the west, From the north and from the south. They wandered in the wilderness in a desolate way; they found no city to dwell in. Hungry and Thirsty, their soul fainted in them. Then they cried out to the Lord in their trouble, And He delivered them out of their distress. And He led them forth by the right way, that they might go to a city for a dwelling place. Oh that men would give thanks to the Lord for His goodness. For He satisfies the longing soul and fills the hungry soul with goodness. Those who sat in darkness and in the shadow of death, Bound in affliction and irons. Because they rebelled against the words of God. (Psalm 107:2–11 KJV)

You may be thinking, "I am not a redeemer of the Lord." I must say yes, you are. He has left none un-redeemed; it was made available to all, and He purchased it. The only thing with the purchase is that you and I have to go and redeem your right to say so! Salvation has been made available to all who call upon His name, and at times we have to allow the Lord to walk us out of those seasons of our lives when we are so focused on, or shall I say distracted by, how much someone else is doing. God has given individuals enough stuff to focus on in their own rights and wrongs, but many choose to add on everyone else's stuff. This is where we have come to the part of my writing of this book to say simply Stop it! Drop other people's baggage. Step away from it, back up, and do whatever you have to do to free yourself from carrying other people's worries and cares.

CHAPTER 3

DEALING WITH THE F WORD

For if you forgive men their trespasses your
heavenly Father will also forgive you. But if
you do not forgive men their trespasses, neither
will your Father forgive your trespasses.
—Matthew 6:14–15 KJV)

You may ask, "How do I see others who may have hurt me
through the lenses of forgiveness and not with the eye's of
unforgiveness and bitterness?" One of the most unspoken

questions among many believers and unbelievers in our houses of faith is what I call the *F* word. Yes, I know; go ahead and say it. "Did he just say what I think he said?" Yes, I did say the *F* word. The only problem is what were you thinking versus what I was saying. The *F* word could be a ticking time bomb in so many relationships right now, whether on a job, with a family member, with a spouse, with a parent, with a friend, in various relationships, and ultimately with our God. I have witnessed the *F* word tear down a lot of things and break apart a lot of marriages and families. I have even witnessed the *F* word carry a lot of souls to the grave without being resolved or exposed. There is one cure and one cure alone: we must do it.

I know you are now saying, "Do what? Do the *F* word? Did I just hear you correctly, Pastor? Are you telling me to go out and do the *F* word? How dare you ask me to do such a thing! You don't even know what that person has done to me. You don't know how many times he or she did the same thing. And you are asking me to go out and do the *F* word?"

Yes, that is exactly what I am encouraging you to do. Simply put, God has commanded you to do it. To get your mind in the right place with your heart so that you may align with His perfect will, you must forgive.

> For if you forgive men their trespasses your heavenly Father will also forgive you. But if you do not forgive men their trespasses, neither will your Father forgive your trespasses. (Matthew 6:14–15 KJV)

Why lose when you and I were created to win? Why lose out on a seat in eternity purchased in blood? All for just a few earthly moments, days, months, or even years with a heart of unforgiveness? May you learn the word, try the word, and begin to live and become one with the *F* word, forgiveness.

CHAPTER 4

COULD I BE A CARRIER?

How about person one forever seeing a problem with something, someone, or even some place? Have you ever run into this particular person? You know—the ones who say that they're not the problem but can quickly identify where the problem is or who is the cause of the problem. Now we have entered the chapter that I would like to introduce to you the reader in which I call the "Carrier." You may have heard the term used medically, and even though my description is far from a medical term, I find it somewhat useful to give similarity to this context. *Disease*

carrier is defined as a person or organism infected with an infectious disease agent but displaying no symptoms. On the other hand, their genetic carriers, for which I use the terms generational cursers and carriers, is defined as a person or an organism that has inherited a genetic traitor mutation but displays no symptoms. I simply choose to use this analogy to explain the person whom I call a carrier.

We have all noticed carriers at one time or another. They're the ones who truly seem to be in the center of everything: drama, controversy, gossip—you name it, and they were a part of it, never taking any responsibility. They're in the middle of every dispute and may bounce from church to church; the same issues they were having at one church now appear at the second church, which is suddenly plagued with the same issues. Carriers always seem to find something wrong with someone or something, challenge authority, and have all the answers to what someone else could do to make the situation better. They draw focus to other people and issues from their own point view. They never take into consideration why it is same issues in different places time after time.

Well, I will let you in on a not-so-hidden secret. If you just so happen to know someone like this or Maybe you find yourself on the other end of this page, saying, "That sounds like me, always trying to get someone to see my point of view, of how someone wronged me, or how much someone else is the cause of this or that." I don't' want to hurt your feelings, but then again, we should not be in our feelings anyway. At the end of the day, have you ever stop and ask yourself, "Am I a carrier? Am I the problem for which I want so many others to take the blame? Am I the cause of much of what I am seeing going wrong, but I'm not realizing it because I bear no symptoms?"

It is time for us to realize that we may be the very center of all that we are blaming others about. Just as in the case of a carrier, even though you bear no symptoms, that does not mean that you are not affecting others. Self-examination is key and very useful when one is faced with church hopping. If the same problems occur at every church that you hop to, then I will be the gander of useful news, the problem may not be within the churches that you are hopping from. The problem may well be in the one who is doing the hopping. I will let that rest where it may. If I have stepped on some toes, it is okay; they will heal. If I have exposed some dark, unrevealed vices, then the light of His Word will lead you to stop hopping in hurt, and you can let the healing begin.

Thy Word is a Lamp to my feet and a Light unto my Path. (Psalm 119:105 KJV)

CHAPTER 5

What is it about Prison that i Did Not Get the First Time? That I had to go back a 2ND or 3RD Time

We have come to a sensitive chapter of this book because it will hit home in so many ways. I am sure you will be able to relate or identify, whether you have someone whom you could relate to or you yourself have experienced the points within this chapter. May the words of knowledge and wisdom released upon the very pages of this chapter find root in some way to create a solution. That seems to be a common problem that many are faced with, and surely, they are in need of an answer.

I will say it is amazing and somewhat of a mystery that I, the author, will not be going back a second or third time to try to regain an answer. What I am saying is that after finding myself in prison for the first time, there was no need to see what a second or third time would bring that I had not gotten the first time around. Now I am left with the burden to challenge you, the reader. If you know of someone who has been incarcerated and seems to be making that door of incarceration a revolving door, then please let the person's eyes gaze upon the words of this chapter. Maybe a small glimpse could shed light upon the critical decisions that they are making to cause them to repeat a cycle that is truly not worth repeating. I have come to find that I know some who have already allowed the enemy to take away their freedom, some for an extended period of time. From the gracious mercy and love of God, they were granted the opportunity to have their freedom once again. For whatever reason, they choose to take that extended love of His grace. After all of the family's heartfelt years of tears and asking God for mercy that loved ones could be released, they turned around and let the same lying devil get them locked back up in the same prison from which God had just set them free.

Now, this is where I pause and want to ask a question. Do you know someone like this? Are you presently dealing with this very issue? Do you have a friend or a family member who never seems to get it? Is the person constantly becoming incarcerated time after time? I want to share a word of wisdom to that individual. I have come to the point that lets me keep it real. Freedom is not enough. It's time to take a closer look at what you are doing and whom you are hurting. Listen! young man or woman that has found this door of incarceration as a revolving door in your life. It is no longer what you are doing to get locked up. It is truly all about whom you are hurting. It's about being selfless, taking this one very moment, and not letting it be about you but rather about the ones whom you are hurting. Case in point, young men and women, But I choose to specifically talk to my young men that are constantly getting locked up even though they have children. I have come to find out in a very harsh reality way that whether it's sons or daughters, as in my case both they do need you there. I clearly remember living in my selfishness and not selflessness. I remember lying to myself while out there hustling and trying to outdo the other men. My son and daughter were just born at the time, but I was out there living in the wilds of life. I wanted to outdo the Joneses, not just keep up with them. I was out there living life fast and risky, lying to myself that my children would not have to need for anything. I sold all that poison to my community. To you all that may be reading and is not that advance in the terminology. I was out there selling all those drugs and placing my children's future in the hands of my foolish decisions. Unfortunately, it all caught up with me, and I need not have gone through all of the destruction that came along with those foolish decisions.

You will find those writings in my first two books, but I am truly choosing to take this opportunity to drive home a point to those out there who have children and are facing the fate of getting locked up. There is no heavier weight that could be placed upon a dad when all of his hopes and dreams with his child growing up has been thrown on the roulette table. It's like throwing our children's future, like a pair of dice in the hopes of avoiding throwing two, three, or twelve in the world of the game called craps. That is about what I did for my son and daughter while I was out there living a street life. The hustle cost me everything, and at the end of it all, that is exactly what I felt like was: crap. Imagine being in a courtroom for you who that are repeat offenders and sitting there ready to get sentenced. The judge says, "Natural life without the possibility of parole." Your two children (in my case, a son and a daughter) are sitting in the courtroom. They were both one year old. Just imagine how hurt I was.

This is the point I want to draw your attention to. It wasn't about how hurt I was. It was about how much I'd just hurt not only one child but two. My selfishness never allowed me to see past myself. I'd simply set the course and made a path of so much hurt for my precious daughter. Now I'd created a misguided path for my son when I should have been teaching guidance. I was handing them over, or shall I say tossing them over, like a set of dice, playing craps with their futures.

My eyes are filled with tears for eighteen years. If only you could hear the passion in my heart. If you have been released from prison, juvenile or county jail don't go back, especially if you have children. Everything you have need of, or shall I say everything that has need of you, is out here. Please don't learn like I had to. You know what I am going to recant the please what I or you look like or sound like asking another man Please don't go back to prison. Please stay out so that your children can have a dad. I said I was going to keep it real, and that is what I am going to do. Young man, little hommie however you want to be address Let's stop hurting the ones who deserve our worth. There is no need to ask please. That is what we as men are called to do: step up, take responsibility, and stop turning the door of incarceration. We should turn the doorknobs to our sons' and daughters' rooms, helping them with their homework and tucking them in at night instead of us having to hear that one shout from the prison guards lights out.

Men, we have to stop contributing to the dysfunction

that goes on in the home because of our absences. The moment the man abandons the home, he sows a seed and a course of dysfunction into that home that is so damaging; it is very hard to recover without the man's presence. Your abandonment of that home causes the trajectory of your son or daughter to spiral out of control. Your missing presence causes your son to grow up without a sense of responsibility, with the absence of any structure or corrective decision making or leadership ability, with any sense of protector attribute; he's surely missing a sense of manhood and pride that every son needs and should get from a father.

Your absence to that home causes your abandoned daughter to grow up without any fatherly sense of belonging and self-worth. She has low self-esteem and seems to be trying to find the access points and crevasses of her heart where your abandonment has caused the feeling of wantonness. Surely the seed of rejection will grow into many misused, misguided, abusive relationships—all because of your decision to abandon that home. It causes that daughter to seek out love in the wrong places, longing for her father's companionship, the one who was to be educator of her values and how to spot the right and wrong feelings when it comes to a boyfriend, all the way up to the point you walk her down the aisle. It causes that daughter to lose the image of what true love is and what a provider and protector should look like. She's searching for a daddy's love—all because the one true figure of such an expression has chosen to abandon not only that home but also that longing daughter who just wanted to give butterfly kisses to her dad. Now she's left for others to take advantage of her lost feelings and confused emotions.

Your abandonment of that home has caused the mother of your children to become something and someone she was not created for, although the woman possesses a strength that is very impressive. Childbearing alone has an unprecedented strength in itself, and there are many other contributing attributes that are impressive. Your abandonment to that home causes a dysfunction in that home that is unbearable, and most of times it's irreparable. Even the mother's strength meets her match. What you have to realize is that a woman was not created to have dual roles. God is a God of order and balance, and because of your choice to abandon that home, you have contributed to destroying that creative balance. That God has planned for it to be Now, please do understand I am not saying that you destroyed God's ability to bring power to such a situation. I am saying that your abandonment has set a course of dysfunction inside the home, which is truly the start of a devastating destruction because the woman was created to do her roles: nurture, love, and provide a tender touch to her children's lives. Man's role was to provide structure, guidance, responsibility, and discipline.

Now we have come to the part of my writings of which I would like to close out with a little something different from my first two books. I want to take this portion to share from other sources of an authentic testimony, which I hope will encourage or inspire someone who can find that we all have a testimony. It may hold the power for someone to overcome, if only it is told. I believe in the power of testimony, and therefore this closing chapter is with an authentic testimony, which I know will inspire many. I conclude this book as I started, with the hope of inspired change to you, the reader. Whether young or old, man or woman, boy or girl, father or son, mother or daughter, incarcerated or free, rich or poor, saved or unsaved, testimonies are how we overcome, they are some small hope of happenstance in the hopes that it will spark a wind for the fire of the Holy Spirit to cause others to share their testimony no matter how small or great they feel that it is. I am a firm believer that there is someone out there who is in need of a testimony to be told. That brings value to the following passages.

> And They Overcame Him By The Blood Of The Lamb And The Word Of Their Testimony. (Revelation 12:11 NKJV)

> "Let the redeemed" of the lord say so. (Psalm 107:2 KJV)

CHAPTER 6

BETTER IS THE END OF A THING THAN THE BEGINNING THEREOF

AUSTIN AVERY III—AUTHENTIC TESTIMONY

The Pursuit of Happiness: Money, Power, Fame, Sex, and Drugs

As far back as I can remember, I've always been a promoter of something: parties, fashion, music, wealth. I've always obtained a certain level of influence in each area. When my parents separated during my tenth grade school year, I decided to take it up a notch. This influence, and lack of parental guidelines, led to me and my crew (who were actually more like brothers) to becoming one of the most popular house party event planners on the Mississippi Gulf Coast (Gautier, Pascagoula, Moss Point, Ocean Springs, and possibly Biloxi too) during that time. At the height of our partying, it was nothing for us to throw an event and have almost everyone from Pascagoula High, Moss Point High, and the surrounding hoods show up, which meant my neighborhood and nearby neighborhoods' streets were gridlocked like Interstate 405 in Los Angeles during rush hour. The fact that members of my family were some of the biggest drug dealers and "street influencers," which meant I had unlimited access to party drugs (mainly marijuana and liquor), didn't hurt.

As my high school graduation day came closer, while my friends were boasting about college plans, I found myself having a conversation with my dad that went something like this. My dad said, "Your mother and I haven't set aside any money for you to go to college. You're eighteen so it's time for you to be a man." I found myself in a navy recruiter's office taking the Armed Services Vocational Aptitude Battery (ASVAB) test. Luckily, I excelled at academics. Scoring an 81 on the test assured that I could go into almost any field that I wanted. I chose aviation administration because it sounded like the job

I could do with minimum effort while stacking a little money.

Fast-forward a few months, and I was headed to boot camp in Orlando, Florida. I was still rough around the edges. I remember arriving to boot camp and getting caught shooting dice in the barracks during the first week. Needless to say, that didn't end well for me (or my entire squadron); we had one of the roughest physical training sessions of the two-month-long stay that day. I quickly realized that I had to carry myself a certain way during normal business hours and then let my hair down at night. I proceeded with those self-given marching orders. I graduated boot camp at the top of my class, excelling in academics and physical training. Upon release from "Mickey Mouse" boot camp, I shipped off to A school in Meridian, Mississippi (approximately two hours from my hometown). I graduated first in my class in A school and then went home that weekend and celebrated harder than anyone in my class. That partying session led to me receiving my first DUI at the age of eighteen. Luckily (at this point I was still attributing the grace on my life to luck because I didn't know the Lord), my dad was able to finesse the court judge with a story about how I'd graduated first in my class, and a DUI on my record would all but end my navy career. The court hit me with a notable fine, and the paperwork never made it to my new command in Norfolk, Virginia.

When I got settled at the Naval Air Station in Norfolk, Virginia, I picked up where I left off, which was carrying myself a certain way during normal business hours and then letting my hair down at night. By this time, I had added another wrinkle to the mix. I had married my high school girlfriend and moved her to a small apartment in the hood in Hampton, Virginia. By day I continued to excel, winning petty officer of the month for the entire naval air station. At night I continued to indulge in underage drinking and clubbing. Did I mention my partying and "do what I feel like" attitude led me to cheat on my wife days before we got married and days after we got married? In fact, I believe the only time I didn't cheat on her was when I did a six-month deployment overseas, and that was only because I was afraid of catching a disease for which America didn't have a cure. I was so naive. My ways eventually led to us separating shortly during my time in Virginia. At that point in time, she started fooling around with an acquaintance of mine, which led to me becoming more reckless than ever.

My nonmilitary crew who also went to high school

with me on the Mississippi Gulf Coast lived in Virginia too, and we couldn't get enough of the streets. In fact, there was a period of time when at least one of us was going to jail every weekend for drinking in public, fighting, or something else. One of those times included me driving down to Atlanta to obtain a black-market gun because I had a beef with some guys in Virginia. After getting the unregistered 9mm, I took a quick nap, hit the slab, and headed back to Virginia with nothing but bad intentions in my mind and heart. Upon arrival, I linked up with my crew for a drinking session followed by a trip to the Virginia Beach strip. But this wasn't any ordinary trip. While en route, I found myself shooting the fully loaded 9mm in the underground tunnel that connected Hampton and Norfolk. Luckily, no one was injured.

In record timing, we found ourselves walking on the Virginia Beach strip. The crew was looking for some action (women), and I was looking for that and more. Before I knew it, I was pulling the 9mm out on random strangers and putting it to their heads, saying, "Get down on the ground and give me your money." I honestly had no intentions on robbing them; I was simply young and dumb and ready to have fun. They didn't know that, though. To the victims, the encounter with me was probably life-altering. That was why most were crying. To me, it was a big joke until it was no longer a joke.

I recall pulling my shirt up and flashing the 9mm to a few women, stunting for them because they were the kind of ladies that liked that type of guy. Then I felt something in my back. I quickly reached for the gun, when I heard my boy's yell, "Slick, don't do it!" I realized I was surrounded by numerous police officers screaming, "*Get down!*" Some of the other police were yelling, "*He has one in the chamber!*" The rest of the night went by like a flash. I was in a holding cell. Then I was talking to the navy representative who was normally onsite at the local jails for idiots like me who found themselves in serious situations. I found myself talking to my senior chief (who fortunately was also from the Mississippi Gulf Coast, Pass Christian). Then I talked to my master chief (she was also from the Mississippi Gulf Coast, Biloxi). In essence, I was surrounded by Mississippi Gulf Coast natives who had my best interests at heart. Lucky, right? Remember, at this point I was still attributing the grace on my life to luck because I didn't know the Lord. Both my senior chief and my master chief said something to the nature of, "Petty Officer Homeboy"—because we were all from the Gulf Coast—"you've gotten yourself in a world of trouble, but we're going to try to get you out of it." And they got me out of it! Still, I would end up with an illegal firearm charge on my record for ten years in addition to being mandated to complete more than one hundred hours of community service (no days or weekends off), in addition to working my standard full-time military shift. I also had to speak to the entire naval air station during a special basewide presentation about the negative effects of underage drinking. I didn't spend any real time in jail. I didn't lose my rank or any money. And I didn't get kicked out of the navy. In fact, I continued to excel in the daytime.

Over the next couple of years, I was transferred to sea duty, where I amassed three Naval Achievement Medals for exemplary service while completing at least one overseas deployment to places like France; Spain; Greece; Koper, Slovenia; Bahrain; Israel; and more. However, I was about to come face-to-face with the consequences of my nightlife. I applied to become an officer, but due to my continuous run-ins with the law, my commander wouldn't sign off on my application. In retrospect, he simply couldn't because my lifestyle wouldn't let him!

Fast-forward a couple of years. I exited the navy and moved my family to Memphis, Tennessee. I called a new city home and embarked upon a new career, information technology. However, I was equipped with the same self-prescribed marching orders: carry myself a certain way during normal business hours, then let my hair down at night. I enrolled in college to further my education, and I graduated with an associate's degree in IT communications and a perfect 4.0 GPA from Southwest Tennessee Community College. Then I went on to Crichton College, where I graduated with a bachelor's degree in organizational management and a 3.8 GPA (I only made one B during my tenure). I was climbing the corporate ladder too. I went from making forty-three thousand dollars annually as a network administrator to sixty thousand dollars as a system engineer to making almost a six-figure salary as a project manager at a Fortune 500 company. I also went from a modest three-bedroom, two-bathroom home with a Galant Mitsubishi car to a two-story, five-bedroom, three-bathroom castle (in my opinion) with a top-of-the-line Cadillac Escalade SUV before I was thirty years old.

At night, I amassed an equally impressive resume. I went from going to strip clubs with my crew every other weekend to cheating on my wife with random women I met at the club every weekend, to staying overnight in hotels with women whom I met (my head count, or should I say bed count, was burgeoning out of control), to separating from my wife and getting my own apartment (while still staying at the house with my wife when I felt like it). But all of that still wasn't enough to quench my insatiable appetite for more money, more power, more fame, more sex, and more drugs.

In 2008, after an opportunity presented itself, I transitioned from my corporate job to pursue a career in the media and entertainment industry. It felt like the right move because my sister was employed within the music industry, and my cousin was Grammy Award–winning Hit-Boy and the Surf Club, blazing trails with major artists in the industry (and the entire Zone 4 camp). Basically, I had two solid inside connections, so I went for it and formed the Memphis Tri-State Record Pool. Our organization's purpose was to connect with all of the up-and-coming regional artists in of a grassroots approach, fostering working relationships among the aforementioned artists and slowly growing our circle and cohesiveness to the point that we could encourage well-known establishments and agencies to provide more opportunities for the artists (e.g., better venues to perform in, better visibility, better pay per events). My business partner and friend happened to be the assistant road manager for a well-known musician artist. We found ourselves using their downtown studio to run our business. Having unlimited access to a downtown studio that belonged to a legendary artist opened up many doors for us. We leveraged that relationship to form solid corporate relationships with the Memphis Music Foundation and the Memphis Music Commission, as well as strong bonds with well-known local artists. As a result, when the Urban Network Conference out of Los Angeles, California, decided to host a conference in Memphis in 2009, we were immediately brought on as media and industry consultants. During that process, I had to travel to Los Angeles to negotiate deals that got Playa Fly and Kinfolk Thugs opening spots for many well-known rap groups. The trip also gave me an opportunity to meet with the general manager at the Hard Rock Cafe. Unfortunately, at that point, I was unable to negotiate a deal with the LA-based Hard Rock Café. For the sake of time, because this is supposed to be a short stroll down memory lane but is becoming a novel, I'll save the story about how one of the California executives laced my drink with drugs (and with what I assume to be "bad and perverse intentions" in his heart) while on that Cali trip. I'll also save the story about how my sister would call me every morning and pray for my protection before I left the hotel.

Instead, I'll focus on how that trip allowed me to negotiate a deal with the Memphis-based Hard Rock Cafe and its general manager. As a result, the Memphis Tri-State Record Pool became mainstays at the Memphis Music Commission's Memphis Music Monday sets while hosting our own Fan Favorite Friday artist spotlight events at the downtown Hard Rock Café. In retrospect, at a young age I realized my words were persuasive and had an uncanny way of opening doors for me. Unfortunately, at this point in my life, they were opening bad doors.

In 2009, although things were looking bright for my partner and me at the Memphis Tri-State Record Pool, my life took a turn. While still riding the wave of a successful Fan Favorite Friday event at the Hard Rock Café a few days earlier and slated to leave for Knoxville or Nashville and then Atlanta with my business partner and a friend that day, I had a moment of clarity. I acknowledged the fact that my current pursuits were garnering me fame and notoriety, but they couldn't feasibly sustain my current lifestyle: spending six hundred dollars a month in gas riding around town, smoking as many as thirteen blunts of premium cush a day, and hanging out in the studio with the local "who's who" in the music industry, eating out up to three times a day, wining and dining multiple women on any given day, and traveling back and forth to the Gulf Coast or Atlanta or California or Florida to my time-share. All of that was coupled with the fact that I was in a battle with my wife to be visible in my three-year-old daughter's life (that situation is a book in itself).

I remember telling my business partner, "I'm giving you everything. One hundred percent equity. You can have access to all the connections we've made. You can have all rights to the website we've built. You can keep any revenue off all the upcoming and future events we have. And I've decided not to make the trip today." To say it was a shock to him would be the understatement of the century. I could see it all over his face as he packed his bags and left the house. I simply had to take a sober look at my life. I locked myself in the house for seven days straight. I didn't answer any calls or entertain any guests. When the smoke from the blunts had cleared and I began to wrap my mind around the recent lack of adequate management of my life and business, I found myself at the end of a divorce that had cost me more than ten thousand dollars and living in an almost empty shell of my aforementioned castle. And the house was about to go into foreclosure. To add insult to injury, the electricity was about to get turned off. I could've paid the light bill, but why would I? The house I'd built in pursuit of happiness—more money, more power, more fame, more sex, and more drugs—was crumbling to the ground right on top of me. In my mind, I had nowhere to go and no one to turn to. I couldn't avoid the fact that it was time for me to man up and face the reality that my choices had created.

At this point, I dusted off the monogrammed Bible that my mom had bought me several years earlier as a

Christmas gift. In those pages, I found hope! And, just like I'd done with the Bible, I started to dust off my life. I didn't tell anyone about my struggles right away. Instead, I started waking up at 6:00 a.m. and reading the Bible uninterrupted until 12:00 p.m. Then I'd take a cold shower (because the electricity was still off), go to Burger King and grab two $0.99 Junior Whoppers, and eat those on my way to Barnes and Noble, where I spent most of the daylight reading the Bible, browsing the Internet, and dodging women. At night, I would go to Walmart to buy candles and a jar of fruit to get me through the night in a house with no electricity. You see, I was in a broken place, but I had started to find my true identity in my newly found constitution, the Bible. I tried to tell my lady friend about the lifestyle changes I was going through, including my promise to the Lord to remain celibate until I found another wife, but she didn't want to hear that. In fact, I remember her response like it was yesterday. After an awkward silence on the phone, she said "I didn't sign up for celibacy. I can't do that!" That hit me hard. Now, when I look back at the situation, I realize the Lord was isolating me so that He could continue to clean me up. This process went on for a month or more.

Fast-forward a few months. I finally exited the foreclosed home. Thankfully, the Lord had allowed me to make a few real estate investments in my past life, which ensured I had a townhome that was paid in full and that I was able to call home for the next two years rent free. I took some of my savings and made improvements to the townhome. Then I took the rest of the money, linked up with a few Gospel rap artists, and went on a multicity tour spreading the good news (the message about the kingdom of God at the level of understanding I had garnered at that time). As a result of one of these tours, I met *my gift,* my wife. We got married in 2010. At that point, she became my *forever wife.* In 2013 we purchased what we thought might be our *forever home* (or at least our five- to ten-year home). Allow me to fast-forward through the rest of the story to date.

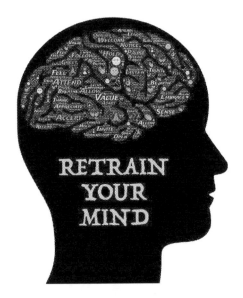

In 2014, my wife and I started to study and understand how the kingdom of God works. I remember taking a shower and hearing the Holy Spirit say we needed to become debt free, which is a kingdom principle. For the sake of time, I'll say that led to me jumping out of the shower and telling my wife, "The Lord told me to sell our two-story home." Now, she didn't immediately believe I'd heard the Lord say that. But over a few weeks, I remember asking her to quit her job to focus on our family vision, knowing this would leave us short on the money necessary to sustain our current lifestyle (**Kingdom of God Key Alert: Operating in Faith—Quitting Job to Focus on Vision**).

I spoke to my employer and stated that I didn't want another raise. Instead, I wanted to receive a percentage off of every website I developed even though our web development division was nonexistent at that time (**Kingdom of God Key Alert: Operating in Faith— Trusted the Lord for an Increase in Finances**).

I promised the Lord that if He grew that web development division, I'd give Him the first fruits of the stipends for each website I developed (**Kingdom of God Key Alert: Being a Giver—Like Abel and Abraham, I Gave the Lord My First Fruits**).

Over time, the Lord made my employer's company the number one web development company in Desoto County.

In 2015, these moves started to pay off. It allowed me and my family to erase approximately twenty-five thousand dollars in debt in nine months, purchase 7.2 acres of land for twenty thousand dollars cash (no loans), and start on the development of what we now refer to as Crown Land debt free.

In 2016, my family was growing. My gift and I welcomed our gift, Josiah Avery, to the world. The Lord was restoring everything that I had previously lost. My family and I were also on the move, as it relates to growing our nonprofit (Fish-N-Loaves), but it was taking us more time than I expected because we were not taking loans. That wait (and spending time with the Lord) led us to relocate our family to one of the most crime-ridden and impoverished zip codes in Memphis, Tennessee, which in urn, catapulted our family vision to reach the hood (**Kingdom of God Key Alert: Being a Servant—Moved from the Suburbs to the Hood**).

In 2017 and 2018, our family vision, which is Fish-N-Loaves and Hungernomics (both aimed at teaching sustainability and eradicating food waste, food insecurity, hunger, and the other attributes associated with oppression and poverty), had started to yield unimaginable fruit.

- Three times a week, we currently pick up excess food from local restaurants and deliver it to residents in some of the most crime-ridden zip codes such as Frayser, Tennessee; North Memphis, Tennessee; and Hernando, Mississippi (West End District).

- Four times a month, we set up a table outside in one of the most crime-ridden zip codes in Memphis, Tennessee (38127) and provide free nutritional food to its residents, as well as talk to them about food preparation strategies.

- Each week, one of our sponsor families delivers free nutritional food to the Fish-N-Loaves Bread Box, strategically deployed in one of the most impoverished communities in Hernando, Mississippi (West End District).

- In less than sixteen months, we've recovered and distributed sixteen thousand pounds (eight tons) of food to those in need, and that number increases weekly.

Furthermore, we're currently in discussions with the American Heart Association on collaborating to do more in the Frayser, Tennessee, communities. We're in discussions with the City of Hernando to do the same thing in Hernando, Mississippi. Our family has also saved and invested seventy-three thousand dollars (which is approximately 90 percent of Phase 1) of a quarter-million-dollar sustainable living community development project that features a 100 percent solar-powered electrical grid, a solar-powered aquaponics community garden that will produce approximately 6.6 tons of produce and fish annually, and modest solar-powered cottages. And we're doing it all debt free, with no loans.

Did I mention, I've also partnered with Royal Chatman (president and CEO of Sources of Intervention Produce Seeds of Prevention) to further his organization's vision? I currently serve as the vice president of public relations and operations. In a short time together, we have begun to expand the organization's reach from Tennessee to Texas. We're currently working to replicate the successes we've witnessed in Tennessee and Texas on the Mississippi Gulf Coast and beyond.

I and my family have purchased more land (debt free) and accomplished so many other things. However, to avoid sounding like I'm boasting, I'll stop here. Like I mentioned previously, as far back as I can remember, I've always been a mouthpiece for something —until I was exposed to the marvelous light that is Christ Jesus. Then I realized that spending valuable time focusing on temporary things didn't add up. I subtracted those things. Now I and the entire Fish-N-Loaves organization don't talk a lot. Instead, we let our actions promote the way, the truth, and the life of the kingdom of God.

The exploits of my life, both negative and positive, have yet to be written in their entirety. Only a Holy Spirit–inspired yearning, coupled with many more days granted on this earth by the Lord, will change this fact.

If there is one point I'd like to get across as a result of this unfinished testimony, it would be that knowing what your gifts are is important because your gifts are what will get you before great men. However, having great character along with attaining knowledge (information) and comprehension (understanding) of the kingdom of God (God's governmental system) and its associated laws (inherent, built-in principles that govern the nature of life and relationships in His creation) is more important.

Chase after gaining knowledge and understanding about the kingdom of God with all your heart because only those who get that knowledge and understanding will truly be successful and have all good things added unto them. It's those individuals who will attain good success and everlasting rule on this earth. I'm not simply telling you something someone else told me, although someone *did* tell me. Neither am I simply telling you something I read, although I *did* read it. I'm telling you something that I accepted for myself, started truly applying to my life in 2009, and seen the abundance manifest in my life at immeasurable levels. This is just the beginning.

About Fish-N-Loaves, Inc.

Headquartered in Byhalia, Mississippi, Fish-N-Loaves, Inc., is a nonprofit organization that believes each soul matters deeply and every life is profoundly significant. As a result, we utilize innovation and creativity to deliver sustainable solutions that address the basic needs of individuals, such as nutritional food and clean drinking water, and we subsequently improve the quality of life within communities. To learn more about Fish-N-Loaves, Inc., please visit http://fish-n-loaves.org.

REFERENCE

AMP

Scripture quotations marked AMP are from The Amplified Bible, Old Testament, copyright ©1965, 1987 by the <u>Zondervan</u> Corporation. The Amplified Bible, New Testament copyright ©1954, 1958, 1987 by <u>The Lockman Foundation</u>. Used by permission. All rights reserved.

KJV

Scripture quotations marked KJV are from the Holy Bible, King James Version (Authorized Version). First published in 1611. Quoted from the KJV Classic Reference Bible, copyright ©1983 by The <u>Zondervan</u> Corporation.

NKJV

Scripture quotations marked NKJV are taken from the New King James Version, copyright ©1982 by <u>Thomas Nelson, Inc</u>. Used by permission. All rights reserved.

Printed in the United States
By Bookmasters